T0381140

Masquerading Memoirs

LAWRENCE CREEGAN

Archway Publishing books may be ordered through booksellers or by contacting:

Archway Publishing
1663 Liberty Drive
Bloomington, IN 47403
www.archwaypublishing.com
844-669-3957

ISBN: 978-1-6657-1048-0 (sc)
ISBN: 978-1-6657-1049-7 (e)

Library of Congress Control Number: 2021915483

Print information available on the last page.

Archway Publishing rev. date: 08/25/2021

In Loving Memory
of a great friend,

Eugene Gino Millekin
GFYB

ACKNOWLEDGEMENTS

<u>Computer & Editing</u>
Brad Gray
Sue Chandler

<u>Photographers</u>
Mark Shortmann
"Candy" Deb Castrovolari

<u>Cover Artists</u>
Jim Cashman
Sarah Riley

Special thanks to the beautiful ladies that allowed me to bring their beauty to a greater level of awareness.

Maggie Carroll King
Nancy "Mama Bliss" Ketner

I'm Larry
Cheers!

MASQUERADING MEMOIRS BY LAWRENCE CREEGAN

This would be my second attempt at creating an avenue for the purpose of entertainment as well as some great ideas in a book. My first book came out in 2004 called "Hilarryous Halloweens" which is the chronological history of my Halloween costumes since the age of six and continuing on until the first book came out with Author House, being the first publisher, hasn't been too successful. This is due to the author being a cheapskate and not spending any money on advertising. I need to sell a few more hundred copies to break even.

My goal is to be on the Ellen DeGeneres show. Perhaps I will have to do some advertising to make that happen. I have continued to make costumes due to the enjoyment I get going out and kicking butt at the local Halloween competitions.

I have to say that in the last few years I have been liking it less and less due to the absence of the friends I have left. They don't want to go to the bars late at night anymore and I can't blame them.

I have won several first prizes over the years in my area and I got used to making that money. In my mind that money became income, so I really had to go out there and bring that money home. It's not like it used to be so I'm thinking that 2019 will be my last costume.

My biggest beef with Halloween nowadays is the music which is typically hip-hop or rap. Today's music offends my seasoned ear for good music. I am an old school rocker and cannot tolerate the younger crowds screeching music. I will bring my own music to bars where I know the owners and they will pacify me by playing it. Me and my white hair have heard other masqueraders who recognize me and say, "when are you going to let someone else win?". When you get that reaction, you know you've done your job well.

With 2019 being the last year I'm going out for Halloween, I have created a pretty cool costume I'd like to call the "**Piece de resistance**". This is my version of a tornado. I thought of it a couple of years ago, but I was dragging my feet making this costume. I realized this year would be my last, so I wanted to create a real good one. This costume has taken months to prepare especially while writing this book. You will see a picture of the tornado later.

The word masquerade is a French term meaning '*to cover up something or participate in something requiring costumes in a theatre setting*'. I said to my friends over the last thirty years that I came in second to last place in the Brad Pitt look-alike contest beating out Charles Manson and that was after he got the swastika tattooed on the bridge of his nose. Even after his reputation and looks after the tattoo, he had some female who wanted to marry him. He died before that could happen.

I think I have this obsession with wearing masks to cover up this mush I'm stuck with. That's probably what the great psychoanalyst Sigmund Freud would probably have said if he were to analyze me. He would have a field day with some couch time with what's bouncing around in my dome. In the last twenty years or so, whenever I meet and intent to ask a female out, I always expect that they will come up with some kind of excuse. I don't feel that I'm very attractive to the opposite sex. I always wonder why women rarely approach me or ask if I am single. We all know that every woman has an available friend, but I never hear "Hey I got a girl for you".

I understand we are all in nature's facial lottery and I didn't do very well which is not my fault nor my parents. It is the Creator of all this stuff called life. When I meet the Creator, who or whatever that may be, I'm going to want to get into a fist fight in retaliation for my suffering…though, I've managed to trick a few women into dating me over the years. They were obviously blinded by love or mesmerized by my personality.

I must stop making this book look like a profile for a dating website. I have cruised dating websites to find out what women want in a man and above all, a great sense of humor, check, next is a good listener, check, would be great if he could cook, check, and handsome, well three out of four isn't bad but no cigar!

Some of my friends and family have offered some advice on writing my second book, saying that even though you have great pictures and stories in the first book and from my point of view a picture is worth a thousand words! Anyway, the general advice was to add more text about some funny things that have happened to me over the years. My relatives say I should immortalize my stories. They also advise me not to name the second book "Hilarryous Halloweens II" and also do NOT put a half-naked picture of myself on the cover as to not scare people away! (I saved it for the end.) So, I went with the classic happy/sad masquerade masks. Not bad advice and I bet they are surprised I took it.

I have some very interesting travel episodes which I would like to elaborate on and maybe you, the reader can chuckle and say to yourself "hey something like that happened to me".

Chapter 1

The Killer Instinct Attitude Continues To Grow

CHAFFING DISH

My memory has as many holes as a 27-hole golf course. I went through the memory process in the makings of my first book asking all my friends if they remembered any costumes I missed. This one was one of the missed costumes from around 1974 I'm guessing. I never remembered this costume until I gave my first book "Hilarryous Halloweens" to my friend Bill to check out. He asked why I didn't put the chafing dish costume in the first book for which I won the Ocean Mist costume party that year.

At that point my memory got jogged and I pulled up that file in my brain. The costume was pretty simple and consisted of an old card table with a hole cut out for my big head and an aluminum baking dish for the dish and another aluminum dish hinged for the top with some onion, carrots and parsley in the pan.

Got some scared people brave enough to lift the lid to find my mush, which is pretty scary, without the dish inside.

STAND-UP BASS FIDDLE

Besides my passion for making costumes, which I start about a month before Halloween, another strong passion of mine is music especially the live stuff, so I thought about the stand-up bass, which I could use for Halloween and another great party at the biggest, coolest ballroom in Rhode Island called" Rhodes on the Pawtuxet." Some promoters call it the Mardi Gras Ball, which is a masquerade ball with prizes, and I thought that a bass fiddle would have a good chance of winning at both affairs.

The first party I went to that year was an old tavern circa 1667 called 'The General Stanton Inn' on the Old Post road in Charlestown, R.I., a place where many a weary traveler would stay going between New York and Boston when Route 1 was the main dirt road traveled and still is a popular tavern and Inn today.

I won first place and after winning I got into my van and slowly sped off to the Narragansett Cafe in Jamestown R.I. I got there in time to be judged and I won first prize there too.

I kept the costume in my shed until the Mardi Gras Ball in February where I took third prize at the ball. All in all, this was a very successful costume year.

GARGOYLES

Being a horror movie buff, I like to check out other people's imaginations. I saw a cheaply made movie called Gargoyles and I did some research on the fabled creatures which are used as decorations for older buildings, pretty spooky architecture. Using my computer, I got several versions of the mighty Gargoyles and came up with my own idea of what a gargoyle looks like. A mix of Pegasus and a unicorn with an ugly horn sticking out of his forehead.

This was a year when Halloween fell on a Friday so there were many parties on the weekend. I again went to the General Stanton Inn in Charlestown R.I. where I won first place. I raced off to the Gansett Cafe and won first place there as well. The next night I placed second at the Mews Tavern. I am pretty sure this was 2005.

CROCKODILE HUNTER

The unfortunate tragic death of Steve Irwin happened in 2006 about a month before Halloween, I don't usually make fun of someone's death, but this guy did flirt with disaster often and the accident didn't surprise me. I was not a fan after I saw him holding his kid while feeding crocs, not too cool. His demise was certain because he would chase animals that could and did kill him.

This was a very unpopular costume among the masses, especially the girls. They made bad comments to me about the costume, even the guys were saying that it was too early to be poking fun with this.

With all the negativity I still pulled in third place. I found out two days later that Bill Maher went to the playboy mansion with a Steve Irwin costume, stingray and all. American comedian Bill Maher has angrily refused to apologize for wearing a bloody Steve Irwin Halloween costume. Great minds think alike!

Maher won't apologize for Irwin costume

SPIDERMAN

Well, nobody's perfect and I would have to say that this was my worst costume.

The idea was to go to a Five K road race they have in the streets of Providence around Halloween time, sponsored by a company called Monster Mini Golf which is a franchised throughout the country. The name says it all. To run in the race, you should be in costume, which draws a lot of ghouls because it's easier to run in that costume and it gave the streets an apocalyptic scene.

I built two miniature high-rise buildings using two high rise buildings found in downtown Providence, one being the "Superman Building", as models. The buildings were the best part of the costume as I needed to attach my wrist webs to something.

This costume ended up being a huge waste of time but is part of the history and must be included. Oh well, that's the way the pumpkin rolls.

BRIAN THE DOG

Raised in Rhode Island, I spent most of my time there outside of a couple of winters in sunny Florida. When the very successful cartoon "FAMILY GUY" came to be, I was head over heels for this show as most of it was based on Rhody humor.

The creator Seth MacFarlane was from nearby Connecticut and went to Rhode Island School of Design and his main writer, Danny Smith, was from Smithfield R.I. I got a big charge from this as their sense of humor was slightly warped and I think we have that in common.

If you can get by the fact that this is a cartoon, it is a very funny series about a dysfunctional family in a made-up town in Rhode Island called "Quahog"

My favorite character is the family's dog, who can speak and is an alcoholic and occasionally has a bag of weed. He is the funniest of all the characters which are all very good, so it's off to the towel store.

I needed two large, off white towels to make this costume with a little chicken wire for the head. The fuzzy side of the towel makes great dog fur hint..hint..; when making this costume make sure the smooth side is inside. I sewed the upper body and had some inside out sweatpants with an added small tail that matched the towels and is reversible, with a brown collar and a gold medal, detail is everything. This was a third prize winner at the Mews Tavern in 2008.

MEWS TREE

When talking to a good friend, Jimmy Z, who has worked at the Mews for years, told me "to win at the Mews you have to be the Mews". He meant that I should go as something that would represent the 69 draft beers, they have on tap there. That is what they are most noted for. I told him he was in the wrong room, the owners Dave and Danny had a vision to making a dining room at their great tavern. They put a real full grown tree in the middle of the dining room, their tree has a real bike, a kayak, a two man saw, and a kite, all of which I had in smaller version of the Mews tree, except for the saw, on my costume. When prize time came, I pulled in a third. I was happy with that as the place was packed with great costumes.

If I were a judge, my costume would not have won anything. There were so many great costumes like the Money with eyes, a popular Geico Insurance TV commercial, who won a well-deserved first prize and a guy who looked better than Johnny Depp in the "Pirates of the Caribbean" movie won second prize, the year was 2009.

POOL BOY

Being into Halloween as I am, I used to watch the Today Show on Halloween to see the different costumes. I heard that The Regis and Kelly Show was giving away $20,000.00 for their first prize for best Halloween costume.

So, I got this huge idea that I could combine the two and go to the Today Show early and then walk over to the Regis show to win some big money. At the time I was working for a friend who lived near New York. I asked him if he would help me with my plan by dropping me and my costume off at the Rockefeller Center with my van and then he was to go and park the van at a near- by underground parking garage and take the train out of there. After staying at his apartment the night before Halloween, we left in my van around 4:00 a.m. and me and the costume were dropped off at the Rockefeller Center. My last words were to him were to" watch out for the roof racks on my van", and off to the garage he went.

It's now about 6:00 a.m. and I'm setting up the costume. I needed a plastic bag for my phone, iPod, cordless screw gun and a can of soda which turned out to be a lousy idea. I was talking to some of the show's tech people, telling them that I was from Rhode Island which the hosts Meredith Vieira and Matt Lauer both had Rhode Island ties. It was about 6:55 AM and I see some camera people moving in to get a closeup and zoom in on me and my costume at 7:00 a.m. I was looking at the huge television on the side of Rockefeller building facing the show, I saw myself on the side of the building, National recognition at last!

After about a half an hour or so it was time to put plan B into effect which was to walk my pool boy costume 22 blocks through midtown Manhattan at 8:00 a.m.

I must have been quite a sight even for Manhattan as I was dragging the costume to get to the Regis and Kelly show and a shot at the big money prize. This is when things started to go badly. Remember the plastic bag with the soda and the electronics? Well, the drill bit pierced the soda can and sprayed the phone and iPod leaving them sticky and wet.

Next, when building the pool frame, I put wheels on the base that were not up to a 22-block midtown Manhattan trip. As I struggled from block to block, pool boy started to come apart. The wheels were failing making the trip a major struggle. After hiking and hour we, me and the pool, manage to get to the street where they have the Regis show, upon closing in on the building I noticed that some people in costume were getting shuffled into the building and when the last costume went in they closed the garage door and I was still about a hundred yards away. I was late NO000000!!!

The main reason for the whole trip was to win the $20,000. After sulking for twenty minutes I left the costume on the sidewalk and took a cab to the underground garage.

On top of that, my friend didn't listen to me when I told him to watch out for the roof racks. As I approached the van, I see that the racks were totally torn off. He had hit the warning bars hanging from the ceiling and kept on going which ripped the roof racks off. Bummed out, I threw the racks in the van and went back to get the pool. It was sitting on the sidewalk, all alone, for about a half an hour in New York City and to my surprise the pool was still there. So, into the van it went and I started back home. I had planned to go to the "Mews" that night, but between my electronics getting wet, being late for Regis and the racks, I had had enough and went home. In eighteen years, I never missed the Mews Halloween party. This was a first for me!

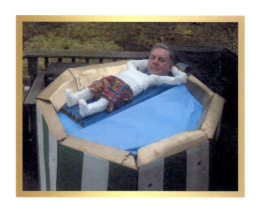

HURRICANE SANDY

In late October of 2012 I had a serious lack of Imagination. I had nothing…totally blank, like writer's block. Then came a crippling hurricane named Sandy which roared up the east coast headed for New England and took a left at the Jersey Shore sparing us. The lightbulb in my head switched on, I had my costume idea at last.

I made a wire structure on my head to hold a white plastic bag with cotton balls glued all over it to look like clouds. I hung a blinking light inside the dome to represent lightning. I was holding a portable fan sprayer for plants to represent rain and I made the thunder sound effects with my voice. I also had a name tag on that said, "hello my name is SANDY". It was not my best and I had to work at the college on that Halloween party night so no prizes but seeing the looks on some of the student faces was worth it. Many selfies.

SEXY TACO

This gem developed in the year 2013. Another year without much of an idea and so one day we served tacos for lunch at the University where I work, I got this idea.

I took perhaps my favorite costume making material which is good old cardboard with a little newspaper fringed up and painted green which provided the lettuce. Then I used insulating foam painted brown to make the beef, which really looked like horse hockey. I did not go on my usual haunts but dressed up for work to get the students reactions and several students wanted a selfie with the sexy taco.

POOP HEAD

In the year of 2014 I got some kind of inspiration from somewhere, it's hard to come up with something to my standards, but this year was different, I first made an ear of corn out of cardboard and a little paint which was cute but not too aggressive and when I heard that the Ocean Mist was giving a thousand dollars for first prize, my killer instincts kicked in and I put my thinking cap on.

Now I still had to come up with a winning costume for the mist party I love using chicken wire and I learned from the sexy taco the year before that painted foam insulation looks more like poop that ground beef, so I wrapped some wire around my head and foamed it and painted it and poop-head was born. Unfortunately, the Mist sold tickets for this event which I was unaware of and the event was sold out by the time I arrived. I sat at the bar next door trying to find a way in, to no avail. I went to five other haunts and couldn't find a contest anywhere.

Sometimes things just be that way.

TITANIC SCHOOL PARTY

At the time of this picture, I was working at the University of Rhode Island, feeding the students. About three times a year the management throws a pretty cool theme party, Carnevale, Titanic etc., which they really go all out and spend a lot of money on many extra entertaining things such as belly dancers, classical guitar player, photo booth, magicians, cotton candy machines and many other things too numerous to mention.

I was privy to the Titanic party a couple of months in advance so I grew my beard and made this costume with things you would find in a kitchen, a chef's coat makes a great captain jacket with some scrambled egg patches on the shoulders. The hat was cardboard covered with a kitchen towel.

The day of the party I donned the costume. The director of dining services liked it so much that he had myself and my lovely co-worker, Nancy who made a hell of an Unsinkable Molly Brown, greet the students as they arrived. The line to get in was about fifty yards long for about two hours.

I knew I would need a prop so I brought an adult toy in the form of a remote controlled horseshoe crab which is a horseshoe crab shell attached to a remote controlled car rolling around the floor near the line of students. There were so many astonished looks on their faces as the crab went up and down the line. This was very funny and so well worth it. This was the most fun I have had at this job. Thanx Nancy you make this picture worth looking at.

EAR OF CORN

For some unknown reason I got a few ideas this particular year and one was from a person on TV dressed as an ear of corn. I said, "I can do that!"

I made it out of cardboard cut and painted to look like corn. I went to work as an ear of corn. The reactions from the students was worth it as it created a selfie opportunity for many of the students. It was fun making it and has to be recognized as part of the history.

HORSES BUTT

Kevin is a friend of mine at the University of Rhode Island. He knew of my skills in costume making so he asked me to make him a costume. I agreed and he left it up to me as to what it would be.

Since he was a little bit of a horse's butt, I decided that Kevin would be a fine horse's butt. Construction began with one of my favorite materials to work with, cardboard, because it is so light, and a steady sharpie created this one. As years go on, light weight is a necessity. I believe Kevin went trick or treating with his daughter in his horse's butt costume, if the shoe fits…...

PINBALL MACHINE

For many years I knew what I was going to be for Halloween the year before. In later years, except for last year I have struggled to think of a costume. I had nothing until I went to my nephew, Ryan's, wedding only to meet Richard, his father in-law, who is not only a costume maker himself,but loves pinball enough that he owns 2 machines which are in his basement. He also rented 2 pinball machines for the wedding reception which was a stroke of genius to have those machines there. It gave all the young people something to do while the adults drank. I recommend this to anyone who is going to throw a wedding.

My pinball was made of cardboard and was light in weight, blinking lights and I got the sounds of a pinball on my phone and ran it through my mini Bose speakers for the bells and whistles. Halloween fell on a Monday. Many places were throwing costume parties all weekend long. The first place went to, the Rathskeller, I won 2nd prize. On Saturday at the Ocean mist I received an honorable mention which means no money and the final night, Halloween, I went to my all-time favorite Halloween haunt only to find out I can't get in because of the size of my costume and I've been in this place in a full size swing set costume before, I don't get it, BUMMED, thanx for the idea Richard!

I took this costume to the Mardi Gras Ball at the coolest ballroom "Rhodes on the Pawtuxet" and was declared the King of the Mardi Gras Ball! More great times.

MINI т-RUMP ON A MISSLE

So, on November 8th, 2016, I received the worst possible birthday present ever, by far, Donald Trump cheated his way to the Presidency of the Country in which I love and live in. I could tell early on that this inept orange buffoon would be a major league disaster.

From what I knew of him from the past and his, for me, was the unwatchable Apprentice show. I wasn't until later on after the election that I realized what a crook he is. I'm really surprised that he thought no one would find out about some of his illegal misgivings.

I've had an idea for a costume for a while of being a tornado which would have taken a long time, of which I was running out of, so I went with the mini-t-RUMP idea. All I needed was an orange Trump wig and a mini missile and I was styling. Trump was having trouble with the North Korean Leader early on in his presidency over practice bombings in the North China Sea with the missiles coming close to Japan.

I had two intensions, first to win and second to make Trump look as foolish as possible, not being a fan at all. 'GET HIM OUT!'

When Halloween came around in 2017, I went to one of my favorite hangs, the "OCEAN MIST". As they were awarding a thousand dollars to the best costume at their Halloween party, I was cruising around the bar, letting the peeps and judges get a look at my Halloween get-up. In my travels around the bar, I must have had fifteen people flip me the bird, you know, the big middle finger, it's a Rhode Island favorite.

It was getting confusing as I couldn't understand if they were flipping me off for chumping Trump or were they flipping me the bird for my character; my guess was, my character didn't like t-RUMP either.

I didn't win anything because big money brings out the real pro costume makers and there were plenty of good ones. I don't mind losing if the costumes are better than mine and that happens all of the time.

The night before the big MIST gig, I took mini t-RUMP to a Southern RI restaurant and won second prize which consisted of a drink on the house.

VULTURE

I got this idea when I went to a friend's beach house party and saw some beach house decorations in the shape of a vulture. I saw someone had taken baby crab claws and small mussel shells that were glued in such a way that the claw was a beak and the shells made the wings with a small piece of cotton ball around the neck which gave this beach decoration an uncanny resemblance to a vulture. I turned this sculpturing into a hobby which I call vulture sculptures, which consists of driftwood I would find on the beach or inland, then mount the driftwood to some Cherrywood flooring and glue these vulture creations all over it with usually a family theme with a nest. The family scene with big and little vultures in a nest scene is the best seller.

So, after years of making and selling these creations I decide to be one for Halloween with good old chicken wire, paper and paint.

Another year that I knew early on at the contests that I wasn't going to win anything because many people started asking me what I was. The idea looked good in my head!

It's never a good sign if you are asked "What are you supposed to be?"

A PAIR OF FUZZY DICE

I was torn on this year's costume as I had a couple of ideas floating around; one, was a tornado, twister, dust devil, or waterspout depending on where you're from two, was a pair of fuzzy dice.

As I like to start my costumes in September, I would have to start midsummer to pull the tornado off. In my mind I would have to borrow all kind of kids toys from my friends who have children, I would have to tell them that their toys will be in a book, Hopefully that will work as I have a twenty dollar limit on costume and If I didn't borrow the items, I would have to pay for those items and would go over my budget. This will most likely be on a future page, as I plan on doing the tornado.

So, I opted to go with idea two "a Pair of Fuzzy Dice"

It was easy enough to make the Dice. Basically, it was two cardboard boxes and a couple of different colored towels. Fairly simple and it showed because I didn't win anything.

It wasn't a bad idea and making them turned out ok but there was NO KILLER INSTINCT and the fact that when two different middle aged women asked me "what are you supposed to be", I knew I was in trouble and wasn't going to win any prize money.

An old saying from my youth applies here "A strong shot that missed the target"

IT'S A TWISTER

Tornados, Twisters, Cyclones, Water Spouts and Dust Devils are all names used for the natural phenomenon when cold, dry air meets warm, moist air, then all hell breaks loose, crazy winds start whirling and spinning to incredible wind speeds capable of major destructive powers, an awesome display of nature.

I've had this idea floating around my head for a few years and didn't do it because I knew how much time it would take to collect all the figurines that would be needed to be ready for Halloween.

As I started asking my friends with children if they had any kind of plastic figurines giving me plenty of time to collect the necessary items to make it look like what I wanted. Of all the figurines that you see in the picture, my favorite one is the neighbor on the "wizard of Oz" who stage name was Almira Gulch the woman on the bike that Toto where jumped out of her basket and she also played the wicked witch of the west. She was the talented actress Margaret Hamilton which brought to light the dangerous powers that these storms can produce.

Who could forget the immortal words "Auntie Em, Auntie Em, it's a twister!"

Chapter 2

TRAVEL GLITCHES

The Bus Ride
European Vacation
Costa Rican Fishing
Scotland Hop
Bumbling Traveler
Graduation

The next few stories of my traveling which I like to call "Travel Glitches".
Which is the author
masquerading around as someone with common sense, logic and sanity.

THE BUS RIDE

One of my earliest memories of travel glitches was when I was about fourteen. One of my best friends and I asked our parents if we could take the transit bus downtown Providence to watch a special movie playing there. My mother gave me enough money for the bus and food from the snack bar.

Well I spent the return bus fare for extra candy. The bus driver was not happy but was kind enough to let me on for free, but I also got a lecture from him for most of the twelve-mile ride. Not too much fun but I think I learned my lesson.

EUROPEAN VACATION

My next recollection of a traveling mishap was in 1969 when my father made arrangements to take the family to Europe to meet my older brother Terry. He was an exchange student from Providence College to the University of Fribourg in Switzerland. My brother picked us up in a Volkswagen bus after an ocean cruise from New York to Le Havre, France. We cruised around Europe for about six weeks.

My Dad had certain places he wanted to see while we were there and one place was Munich Germany. He wanted to go see the famous Glockenspiel which is kind of an alarm clock built on the side of a building that goes off at certain times during the day. It is built from thirty-two marionettes and forty-three bells that come out to dance and spin. Then near the end of a fifteen-minute show, there is a dual between two factions of Germany. It's a jousting match between Bavarian jousters represented by their white and blue. They are the old foe of Lothringian who are in white and red.

After we had seen the glockenspiel do its thing, we started walking away in a very crowded area of which I took the lead. I looked back and noticed that I didn't recognize anyone behind me. So, there I was in an unfamiliar city, I didn't know where the hotel was, didn't have much money, didn't speak German and cell phones weren't invented yet. This awful feeling of uneasiness come over me. I kept on walking and walking until I was finally reunited with my kin. I don't know how much time passed but it seemed like forever.

Then to Ireland for a week and then a flight to England for four days. From there we took a five-day cruise on the ocean liner SS France back to New York. During the trek home we hit the tail end of a hurricane which had 25 to 40-foot swells. Not much fun for that part of the cruise, seasickness was ever prevalent, but it was still the best trip I was ever on.

COSTA RICAN FISHING

I don't have the money to travel extensively but I have gotten around. I've been six times to Costa Rica. An old friend developed a hotel on the south side of Drake Bay, Costa Rica where he runs fishing, diving and hiking tours from his hotel on the edge of the jungle. I suggest you put Aquila de Osa Inn on your bucket list and ask for Brad.

I've traveled to Ireland twice, Scotland once, and England once. I traveled around the United States twice only missing Hawaii, Alaska and Arkansas, maybe someday.

When fishing at my friend Brad's fishing camp and hotel, there is a certain lore, customs and unwritten rules that go along with the whole experience. First, you have to bring your own cannabis medicine, as the cannabis medicine they have there is very good from what I've read.

The day starts promptly at 4:00 AM with the howler monkeys. They are your alarm clock. They come down from the deep jungle to let you know that they are up, and they want you to be up as well considering the volume of the howls.

Next is to shower, dress for fishing and then be at breakfast for 6:15 AM. You are out on the Pacific Ocean by7:00AM. At about 7:15 we have to stop to take care of the Captain's hangover with a little USA cannabis. It's good to keep the Captain in top physical condition.

Then we to go look for some food fish such as tuna, dorado a.k.a. mahi-mahi, cobia and wahoo to name a few. After a while of trying to catch dinner, it was out to deep sea fishing for trophy fish like sailfish and marlin. We spent a couple of hours at that then back to food fishing on the way back to the dock. The catch goes to the chef where he will prepare whatever you caught; however, you like it. Some of my favorites are wahoo, sashimi and dorado in a light teriyaki sauce.

Sometime during the meal Brad will explain to the rest of his guests that myself and my friends were responsible for the nights' dinner. which brought us a round of applause from the guests for the fishermen came back and fed them such a bounty from the sea.

On one trip, after taking care of Willie the Captain's physical problems, we set out to find some fish we could feed the guests when after a minute of running out to the fishing grounds the Captain stopped the boat, hopped down off the flying bridge, signal to the mate to give him a rod, casted a ballyhoo off the port side and hooked a rather large dorado.

He then handed the rod to my friend Dave to fight the fish within minutes of leaving the dock. We had enough fish already to feed all of the guests at the hotel. I was very impressed.

Some classic glitches happened on the way to and from Costa Rica for our fantastic fishing trips with Brad. The first was when I went with two good friends Charlie and Dave. We planned to go down on a Saturday and be at the resort on Sunday.

Then we would fish until Tuesday and leave on Wednesday. For some reason I had in my mind that Thursday was the day to leave. The fishing was great. We caught some really big fish. On Wednesday Charlie said he was having so much fun that he wanted to change his return date. He called the airline on Wednesday only to find out that we were all supposed to leave that day, so we all had to change our tickets. It cost a little extra to change the flight plan and my friends were not mad at me for the extra cost and we remain friends to this day.

My glitches must've rubbed off on a couple of friends in Costa Rica. Both having left their passports with friend Dave. When he got out of the cab in San Jose in Costa Rica his passport had slipped out of his luggage without him noticing. I was the last to get out and noticed it on the floor of the cab. I picked it up. It took a few minutes to get to the hotel. I asked Dave where his passport was. He couldn't find it and while he was looking frantically, I pulled it out of my pocket. He was so happy he bought drinks the whole evening. Now, Jimmy wasn't so lucky. He misplaced his passport in the room at the hotel when it fell out of his luggage and it slipped behind some padding that he didn't notice.

This was our last day, so we left Drake Bay to catch a plane to the States. Jim could not find his passport, so he had to go to the United States Embassy in San Jose to pick up a temporary passport that cost $77. Jim only had $74 dollars to his name so he went around the embassy to bum $3 so he could get his passport in order to leave the country.

We weren't sure that he was going to make it before the plane left. He had two hours to get it all done and get to the plane. I didn't think I was going to see him when right before the plane closed its doors he came walking on with a big grin on his face. He really didn't want to spend another night at the hotel. He was already $3 deep to a total stranger at the embassy.

Great memories! I've been to Brad's hotel six times and hope to get a few more fishing trips in. It's a boat load of fun – no pun intended!

SCOTLAND HOP

After the Costa Rica trips, I went to Edinburg Scotland to help one of my best friends fix up his flat on Montgomery Street in Edinburgh during the Edinburgh Festival in August. Did I mention that I am a general contractor by trade?

We had a flight from New Jersey to London and we had to take a commuter train to the terminal where the plane was. As I got off the com- muter train and walked a few steps I realized that I had left my brand-new camera that I bought just for this trip, on the train. I said some- thing to my friend who immediately went back to the train to retrieve my camera.

During the short time he was gone I went through every horror scenario especially the picture of my friend and camera heading back to the main terminal or to another plane in which we were going to miss our plane. I was so relieved to see come back with my camera as I heard I would need a camera for sights that I was going to see at Edinburgh Festival. The Edinburgh International Festival is a month-long celebration of all kinds of street performers.

Definitely put this festival on your bucket list of eye-popping sites.

THE BUMBLING TRAVELER

For my 6th trip in so many years, I made travel arrangements to leave Green airport at 6:00 am which meant getting up at 3:50 am to get to the plane on time. Upon arriving at the airport, we checked in the baggage, in which I had pulled a bone head move of putting my passport in the check in luggage. I showed my license and boarding pass and on the plain I went.

When I got to my connection flight in Atlanta, they asked for my boarding pass and passport. I told them that I put my passport in my check in luggage. They send a Delta employee baggage handler to find my bag among the luggage to retrieve my passport. While this is happening, the plane is held up for 20 minutes with 270 people wondering why.

I asked the woman at the desk how often this happens, expecting her to say: "All the time". NOPE!! She said around once a year. At that point I felt pretty small. I had to reach up to get out of my sneakers. She then informed me that the pilot and crew wanted to know who I was, the people on the plane wanted to know who I was, the ground people wanted to know who I was, the pilots and crews in the air waiting for a gate wanted to know who I was. It took 25 minutes to find my bag and retrieve my passport and I boarded the plane. As I walked down the aisle, I informed every row that "it was me, it was my fault the flight was delayed", yup, "it was my fault" and I said this to every row until I got to the back of the plane where my friends were. They were hiding in their seats, pretending not to know me! I greeted my friends, much to their chagrin and told everybody that they were with me!

My happy ending is that I caught a really big fish and then got home safely, only to find that the battery in my van was dead.

GRADUATION

Now, most of my travel blunders are purely my fault but the last glitch happened to me when I went to my great-nephew's college graduation from the great school of Northern Arizona State University; which is located in Flagstaff Arizona, home of the lumberjacks (how did I get so old so fast).

My plan was to fly in a day early to Phoenix and take a shuttle bus to Flagstaff. I had been texting my great-nephew in the airport telling him to find a nice place for dinner and we would watch a Celtic playoff game. On the way to Flagstaff the shuttle bus driver let me borrow a charging cord as my phone had little juice. When I got to my hotel, I tried to contact my grand-nephew and found my phone was completely dead. It wouldn't power up and it wouldn't take a charge. The phone was only five months old! All of my contacts were in the phone and now I had no way to get in touch with my grand-nephew or anyone else. They had a house already rented and ready to go but I didn't know where it was located. I felt hopeless so I went into my wallet to get my address book out and low and behold it wasn't there. So, I went to the hotel, no dinner, no Celtic playoff game and I'm totally bummed!

I couldn't get in touch with my nephew as his number was locked in my dead phone. I'm sure he was wondering what happened to me as our communications abruptly ended.

The next morning, I called a cab to take me to Best Buy to buy a new charging cable. I didn't think it was the phone because it was new. I asked the store clerk if I could plug my phone in while I was there just in case. It didn't work; so off to a phone store I go in the cab. When I got to the phone store, I gave the phone to the technician he hooked it up to a diagnostic and charging system of which neither worked. The technician then asked me if I knew that there was a recall on that particular phone. I said "No". I asked if they would sell me a new phone only to inform me that the contacts could not be copied over.

So, I'm back to square one with not having any phone numbers! I need the numbers in order to find the rental where everyone is staying!

I plug in the new phone and I start to get messages from people who were concerned about my whereabouts. As the messages came in so did the phone numbers. I was so relieved and as soon as the phone would let me, I called my nephew to let them know what had happened. He was relieved and we all got together. I had a blast for the rest of the week. I had my contacts backed up on my computer at home, so I was able to restore them all.

Chapter 3

Dress-capades
Chowder Cook-Off
Sparky

DRESS-CAPADES

One of the reasons I decided to move to Block Island was because one of my friend's parents from Warwick, Geno, had property there. The quarter acre lot sat behind the liquor store on the main drag. At one time it was the livery stable and carriage repair. A field stone building sat towards the rear of the property which was about twenty-four feet long and twelve feet wide.

My friend Geno decided that he would move into this building which was appealing to him because there was no rent involved. There was no running water, no toilet, no shower, but he made it work. He carried in gallons of water and a ship's porta-potty which took care of everything. A very funny place to hang out as all of the major characters of the Island would come to visit.

Geno's property divided the liquor store's parking lot. Geno was particular about his side of the lot. Geno was also one of the liquor store's best customers, so he walked a fine line with the parking. He wanted NO TOURISTAS on his side of the lot. One busy, hot summer day a tourista parked on his side of the parking lot. Upon noticing that a tourista had broken the unknown rules, Geno called to get the car towed. They told him that they were too busy to respond to such a frivolous complaint. Geno told the dispatcher that he would be seeing someone soon enough.

He then drove his van up to the rogue Jeep and put a chain on it and towed the parked Jeep to the middle of the road in front of the liquor store. He was right, someone showed up and after seeing what had happened, they ended up charging Geno with disorderly conduct. Geno had to go to the mainland to go to court weeks later to answer the charges from the Block Island affair.

He got on the ferry to go to court, now Geno was a house painter and it was summer, so Geno went to court in painted work shorts. There was a big sign on the court room door "No Shorts Allowed' which meant no Geno allowed. On the way back to the ferry he stopped at another good friend's house who lived near the ferry. After Geno went to court to get the bad news about the short's situation, I happened to be there when he showed up.

He was swearing up a storm about judges and courtrooms. After he worked himself into a lather, I convinced him that he could be allowed to go to court in a dress which he agreed. So, he put on a dress. I found a coon skin hat and I had a camera! I snapped his picture which I immediately made several copies (no digital) and sent copies to all of his relatives.

Geno never did go to court in a dress and coon skin hat, probably for the better, but the whole affair was so much fun. I miss those days.

Thanks Geno. RIP, you are missed.

CHOWDER COOK-OFF

In the early days of summer in Newport RI, Corporations used to sponsor chowder cook- offs in the downtown area. Now me being a culinary arts graduate from Johnson & Wales College in Providence RI. A classmate came up with the slogan I wish I came up with 'BAM! Let's kick it up a notch!'

I have a bit of imagination and I like to win money. Growing up by the ocean on Narragansett Bay, we learned how to get clams early and I acquired a taste for the rubbery slugs as well as for just about anything that comes out of the sea. I'm a big fan of clam chowder. I prefer the milk chowder, New England, as opposed to the tomato base or Manhattan chowder or the clear broth chowder known as Rhode Island chowder.

A friend of mine from my hometown is a fisherman in Narragansett and he would often leave me a bucket full of seafood and ice. No matter what he gave me. There were always clams at the bottom of the buck-et. All I had to do was to make something yummy and share with him. He's a better fisherman than he is a cook.

After making several regular batches of New England clam chowder I was getting bored, so I decided to experiment. I am a lover of the tartness of the cranberry and the bite of a jalapeno pepper so into the chowder they went. The cranberry turned the cream a pinkish color and the jalapeno gave it a zip. I call the chowder Creegan's Cranberry clam chowder or C4 like the military explosives. I would bring my chowder to friend's parties, cookouts and my own St. Patrick's Day parties with rave reviews. Again, the light bulb went off and I decided to enter my recipe in the Newport Chowder Cook-off. I got the rules for the cook-off a couple of weeks before and I broke the first rule right off the bat. All cooking must take place in a kitchen that can be inspected by the Health Department. I made ninety gallons of C4 on the back deck of my house, oops.

I had a fifty-gallon pot that I borrowed. It was big enough to take a bath in. I made two batches of the chowder. The organizers suggested that the participants make 100 gallons to have enough to feed the masses of people going through the chowder cook-off. They expected twelve thousand people going by twenty-six different booths serving one-ounce cups so if you went and tried one from each booth you would have eaten a lot of chowder. Anyway, I needed to have a restaurant name in order to enter so a good buddy of mine who runs a small café not far from me. On occasion I would work for him if he needed a fill-in. In the early 90s my friend agreed that I could use the name of the restaurant, Wiley's, for which he had to be a taster and a voter for the cook-off.

Now I needed some volunteers to help pull this chicanery off. I think there were nine of us, three of my hot lady friends and five guy friends. They were retrieving chowder, making sure it was hot and that the three crock pots I was serving from stayed full which allowed me to stand in front of my booth and do a meet and greet.

Out of the twelve thousand people going through, three people stood out in my mind. They all had jarhead military haircuts. I pegged them as Navy Seals. My booth was the last of 16 in the clam category. I heard one of the Seals say loud enough for the booth next to me to hear that they had tasted the worst chowder. I was talking to them as they were tasting my chowder and asked what they did when one of them said very casually "we kill people". "OK" I said and his reply was "we mainly stick to the enemy". I asked, "how about Irish chefs?" They assured me that I was safe because my chowder was really good.

The competition part of the cook-off was a one thousand-dollar first prize for the clam category and a lot less for second and third prize. The creative and seafood categories were about half the money as a clam category. I was a little cocky and went for the big money. I think I would have won if I had entered into the creative category. I came in sixth place, but I was very proud at beating out a lot of those restaurants.

Although I didn't win any money, speaking for all who helped me with this adventure, we had such a blast with the whole experience. When I see these friends nowadays, they always ask if we're going to do that again and if so, can they help.

We all had a lot of fun. The stories in this book are some of the great memories that stick out in my life.

SPARKY

Last, but not least, I must tell you how I got my nickname "Sparky".

In the early 1980s I got my nickname on Block Island. A few of my friends and people from my hometown had moved there so I had a base. I went looking for a job and a place to live. I was fresh out of culinary school I got a job at the National Hotel on the main drag of Block Island as the Chef. I believe I got the job in May and the owner gave me a room on the fourth floor. This was Block Island, so nobody cared as living quarters for workers was pretty tight in the summer. Lots of jobs with no place to live, so there I am working as a Chef with a room included. I'm thinking life is pretty grand.

After six weeks of getting all of my fellow workers and the guests loving the food coming out of the kitchen, I thought I was gold! On Friday, June 17th, the owner came up to me and said he wanted to meet me after my shift. I honestly thought that because things were going so good and that he was going to give me a raise. Instead he fired me, truly blindsided me. When I asked him why I was getting fired, he claimed I wasn't keeping the kitchen clean enough which was the responsibility of the senior dishwasher. The real reason was that I was a temporary chef until his summer staffing arrived.

The owner, at that time, said that I could stay in the room for one more night, but he had someone moving in the next day. I knew from that point no matter what kind of job I did, he had a whole crew ready to go and I was going to get the axe no matter what. After leaving my job for the last day, I went to help someone work on a boat and waited for the guy who just fired me. He was a fellow Irishman who was headed to open up his bar to have a summer St. Patrick's Day party with an open bar and that, I was not going to pass up. I got cleaned up and went to the 7:00 PM open bar. Around 7:45 PM a cop on the porch was checking IDs. A girl who was living on the fourth floor, down the hall from me, suddenly ran up to the cop and had a small conversation upon which the cop yelled to everyone in the bar to get out.

Everyone kind of looked at each other and no one moved until the cop yelled much louder to leave the building as there was a fire developing on the fourth floor, the floor I lived on. When I realized that I was outside and my possessions were inside my room three doors down from the fire, I wanted to go in and retrieve my stuff. I was refused entry so all I could do was hope the fire didn't burn it all.

The Block Island fire department came and saved the building which had previously burned down in 1904. They saved the building along with my worldly possessions as this would help me later on in the story. After the fire was completely out, I went to a couple of drinking establishments and an after-hours party. Then they allowed me to go back into the building to stay for my last night. It was close to 4:30AM by this time so I went to my room to sleep the night off. The room I was in has high ceilings and kind of a small passageway going through to the hallway allowing air to come into the room. I really don't know what its purpose was, so I took my clothes off and laid on the bed not noticing that the bed was covered in soot. I woke in the morning, a couple of hours later, I looked into the mirror to find my whole body had turned black overnight. I was covered head to toe in soot. Quickly, into the shower I went, laughing all the way before anyone could witness this hilarious scene, and washed off the soot.

After packing up my room to leave for the last time I went downstairs to the kitchen to collect my belongings which included music and my knives. I ran into the owner there and he informed me that the local authorities wanted to talk to me.

After the first ferry docked a man introduced himself as an Agent from the State or something like that. He was the State Investigator and he instructed me to take a ride with him to the police station for some interrogation as the first question asked at the hotel was "had anyone been fired recently". The owner told him I had been fired the day before and off to the police station we went. I was in a room with the Investigator, a State detective and Block Islands finest, who were all asking me questions like, who are my friends on the island, have I ever blacked out from drinking, lots of questions about drinking.

After about forty-five minutes of questioning, I had a question for the people interrogating me. My one question was to look me square in the eye and tell if I looked crazy enough to light all of my possessions on fire which were in my room at the time. I explained to them that they had to let me go because I didn't have a job or a place to live and I needed to find both. They let me go temporarily so they could go and pick up the friends that I told them I knew on the island. They wanted to ask them all if I was capable of lighting a crowded hotel on fire. The answer they got was 'NO Larry was not capable of doing such a thing'. Arson carries a sentence of thirty-five years in jail. After the interviews with my friends, Block Island's finest picked me up again for more questioning.

When we were alone, it was explained to me that I could get off easier if I were to confess to this hotel fire, saying that they knew I lit the fire as revenge for getting fired. I told them where they could stick their theory and I was sticking to my story. Then they asked if I would take a lie detector test and I said I would to prove my innocence. They let me go saying something about blah, blah, blah and setting up a polygraph test for me in about a week in the town of Narragansett, RI where the ferry takes off from. I conveniently forgot about this until the night before the polygraph that was to be set up in Narragansett. Block Island's finest let me know that I was to get on the ferry on the very next morning. I explained to them that I didn't have a job so I couldn't afford the fare. They told me that the State would pick up the round-trip ticket. After they purchased the ticket, I got kind of a cold sweat and sick to my stomach as stuff was getting real at this point. Before getting on the ferry I called my lawyer for the first time and told him my story.

He advised me not to go to the police station unless I was under arrest and then explained to me that if it should happen, we would sue. I got on the ferry and when I got to Narragansett there was a detective waiting for me. I introduced myself and told the them what my lawyer had explained to me. I asked if I was under arrest. They said they didn't know and would have to find out. The detective I was talking to asked if I would go to a pay phone to speak with him so that it wouldn't go across the police airwaves.

Again, I had to explain to the detective that I had not even a dime for the phone, so he accommodated me, and I was on the line with the detective. He explained to me that the State Police had set up the lie detector test at the Narragansett Station and I had a 9:00 AM appointment. I told the detective that my lawyer advised me not to come to the station unless I was under arrest. The detective asked me if I knew that the State had spent a lot of money setting up the polygraph test. He then asked, "Why did you wait until you got to the other side to let us know that you weren't going to come here today?" I told him I needed a free ride to the mainland and back.

This made him very angry and he said before slamming the phone down "We will be talking to you again Mister Creegan!" I never heard from them again.

I spent the next winter on the island and next summer rolled around. There was another small innocent kitchen fire at a hotel two doors down from the National. The State sent their State Investigator again to investigate this innocent grease fire. Nothing to do with arson but he had to investigate it anyway. He was on the last ferry back to the mainland and it just so happened that I too was on that ferry.

At this time there were no Coast Guard regulations about civilians riding in the wheelhouse with the Captain, so being the Captain was a personal friend I would often choose to ride with him, no tourists.

The Investigator who apparently rolled with the Captain on the way over to investigate the fire had asked if he could ride in the wheelhouse and the Captain being a nice guy, agreed so I was on one side of the Captain and he was on the other. I could tell for the hour-long cruise that he knew who I was but just couldn't place me.

The boat let us off in Galilee. I had arrangements for a ride to the nearest main highway about four miles north from the ferry. We then parted ways because they were headed south, and I was going north.

I stuck my thumb out and the first car pulled over and let me in was my old friend the State Investigator. As we were driving along, he asked me where I was going. I explained that my father lived in Warwick. He said he lived in the next town over in Cranston. After some small talk he said that he recognized me but couldn't place me from where. I explained to him that he investigated me with the National fire the summer before where I got the nick name "Sparkie".

He got a chuckle out of that and I said that I guess you guys figured out I didn't light that fire. He agreed that they kind of knew when I explained about all of my possessions were in the room at the time of the fire and all of my friends vouched for me. He gave me a ride right to my father's door.

Thanks for being a great guy my old friend. You did your job well as you didn't find an innocent man guilty.

I ended up finding out who did start the fire. It was a drug deal gone bad and the perp has since passed away. As a result of this whole escapade, the nickname Sparkie stuck. I've been using this nickname as a handle for CB radio in the Block Island Taxi which was my next job. The nickname also became my email address though I spell it differently. Many of my Block Island friends still call me Sparkie to this day.

I'm pretty good with a needle and thread and knowing how to sew which my Mom taught me how to do at a young age, I took a National tee shirt and embroidered flames and smoke coming out of the window of the arsonist's room with the name Sparky and the date June 17th all embroidered on the front. I still wear it on occasion although it's wearing out, everyone still gets a big charge out of this tee shirt except the owner, at that time, of the National Hotel.

THE END for now…

THE CHAPTER THAT SHOULD NEVER HAVE HAPPENED

Well, in my mind this book was finished by Halloween 2019. I advertised on social media that the book would be ready for pursuing as I wanted the book ready for Halloween 2019 to help sales perhaps. Wow was I wrong! My publisher had other ideas as they had big problems with my text due to libelous and slander verbiage that they said occurred in some of my stories (being too truthful I suppose). There might have been some people who might have come back to sue me and the publisher, so I revised some stories to keep them happy.

So, while I am working on jumping through hoops to avoid being sued, around April 2020 I had some developing medical things happening. I had a sinus issue that would not go away. I went to the doctor and he cut out a polyp from my right nostril and sent if off to be tested. The test came back positive for melanoma cancer. It had developed under the skin which, of course, is rare and forced me to take an early retirement from my job twenty-four days earlier than I originally planned.

Meanwhile, going through eight hours of facial surgery and a bout of radiation and chemotherapy, Halloween fell on a day between surgery and radiation. I got home two days after surgery and was home about five minutes and a woman pulled up in a pickup truck I had never seen before. She came to the door and was greeted by a guy with staples and stitches all over his face. I asked her if I could help her. She asked me "are you all right?" and I explained my surgery story. Then she asked me if I wanted to be in the Halloween parade with my rare vintage Swedish sports car which is well liked among my neighbors. I told her if I felt up to it I would love to be part of the parade and I did.

After the parade I had to go home and get my what I'm going to call "hillbilly distancing candy shoot". It was a rain down spout attached to my storm door. It was at the right height for trick or treaters to get their treat. I didn't get many kids after the parade, but the kids and their parents all loved my dispenser.

My Workshop

ABOUT THE AUTHOR

The fourth son of Irish schoolteachers, Lawrence Creegan inherited his parents' sense of whimsy and fun. He grew up in Warwick, Rhode Island where he graduated from high school in 1973.

Larry attended Johnson & Wales University, earning an Associate Degree in Culinary Arts in 1978. He began his many adventures after graduating, from snowbird treks at ski resorts around the country to balmy Florida winters. In 1982, he moved to Block Island for four long years on "the rock" where he cooked, tended bar and worked construction.

Larry wandered the country again and eventually settled on Rhode Island's southern coast where he began a successful home remodeling business and chefs himself out when he needs a change in venue.

Larry is an avid fisherman, loves music, concerts and traveling. True to his New England roots, he is a diehard Red Sox, Patriot and PC Friar Basketball fan. Larry finds himself invited to many unusual parties because of his outrageous outfits – and because he always brings something really special to eat!

Larry is well known for always having a good joke to tell and has dedicated his life to making people laugh.

As his first book illustrates, Larry has also raised Halloween costuming to an art form.

UNIQUE SEASHORE SCULPTURES

Everyone has connections to the sea. Mine is to recycle items found on the beach and to design sculptures related to the seashore.

If you have any interest in building any costumes from this book or my first book, "Hilarryous Halloweens" for yourself, feel free to contact me for detailed instructions for a nominal fee of $10.00.

Larry Creegan
Narragansett, Rhode Island
Webpage – creeganscreations.com
Email – sparkqui@gmail.com
PayPal – paypal.me/sparkqui

Make your library complete, pick up a copy of
Larry's first book; "Hi-Larry-ous Halloweens" from the publisher "authorHOUSE"

"All who own one are happy!"